How Do We
Eat It?

How Do We Eat It?

Deborah Pedersen Vanderniet

Deseret Book Company
Salt Lake City, Utah

First printing April 1982

Library of Congress Cataloging-in-Publication Data

Vanderniet, Deborah Pedersen, 1953–
    How do we eat it?

    Includes index.
    1. Cookery (Cereals)   I. Title.
TX808.V256   641.6'31   82-1420
ISBN 0-87747-905-4   AACR2

Printed in the United States of America   72853-6501

10   9   8   7   6   5   4   3   2

To my husband Clark, whose encouragement, appreciativeness, and pride in me make homemaking such a rewarding career

CONTENTS

INTRODUCTION

"All grain is ordained for the use of man and of beasts, to be the staff of life. . . . All grain is good for the food of man." (Doctrine and Covenants 89:14, 16)

As a concerned homemaker, you are probably well aware of the nutritional and economical value of wheat cookery. Few home-baked items can match the wholesomeness, the taste, or even the emotional and psychological impact of the delightful scent from a loaf of wheat bread straight from the oven.

But if you've limited your use of whole grains to wheat, you've yet to discover a world of delicious meals using millet, oats, rice, soybeans, and other grains. They are relatively inexpensive, and there are many delicious ways to serve them.

Economy is just one reason to use whole grains in your meal planning. Good nutrition is another very important one. Delicious, natural grains, just as they come from the earth, are far superior to those that have lost their nutrients through milling and processing and are then "enriched" with artificial vitamins and minerals. Milled grains also lose their "roughage," a food element being discussed more and more in connection with proper digestion.

The key to successful whole grain cookery is to prepare meals and snacks your family will truly enjoy. No matter how economical or nutritious your meals are, if your family doesn't like them, they are useless. We can't expect our families to eat meals simply because they are good for us; it helps if they are also delicious. Many of the following recipes have been a real hit, even with the most devout meat-and-potatoes lovers.

Many recipes in this book can be adjusted according to taste—adding, increasing, or reducing one or more ingredients. Sunflower or sesame seeds can be added to casseroles; chopped nuts or soy nuts can be added to or omitted from desserts; the amount of meat or poultry in main dishes can be increased; herbs and seasonings can be adjusted to personal taste, and so forth. It is important to not be afraid to adjust the amount of whole wheat flour or rolled oats to obtain the desired texture. Because the moisture content and texture of grains vary, this may be necessary. If cookie dough seems too dry, beat in a little more margarine or a few teaspoons of milk; if cake batter seems too thin, beat in a little flour. One word of caution: baking powder breads such as biscuits, muffins, and banana breads may toughen after too excessive beating. Otherwise, be flexible. Once you have acquired a knack for cooking with grains, you'll be able to create and modify your own favorite recipes.

If you do not own or have access to a wheat grinder, don't let that stop you from using wheat or other grains. There are several alternatives to grinding grains into flour. You can cook them whole, crack them, or sprout them. Instructions for all methods are included in this book.

WHEAT

If you are trying to find ways to feed your family delicious and nourishing meals while at the same time stretching your food dollar, you may have already discovered the economics of wheat—a lot of nourishment for very little money. Wheat contains vitamins, minerals, roughage, and protein; indeed, it is, and should be, the "staff of life." How very appropriate it is to use wheat in its various forms as main dishes, side dishes, snacks, and desserts. If you've limited your use of wheat to breads, then you have not yet discovered the delights of the endless variety of delicious meals you can prepare.

Cooked Wheat

There are several ways to cook wheat. Here are three:

1. In a pan, bring one part wheat and two parts water, with ½ to 1 tsp. salt, to a boil; cover, remove from heat. Let stand overnight (at least 10 hours).

2. Put one part wheat and two parts water in a pan with ½ to 1 tsp. salt. Bring to boil; reduce heat and simmer gently for 4 to 6 hours or until tender.

3. Combine one part wheat and two parts water with ½ to 1 tsp. salt in a crockpot or slow cooker. Cover and cook 4 to 6 hours.

Cooked wheat can be stored up to 2 weeks in the refrigerator.

Tip! Add cooked wheat berries to bread dough for an unusual wheat berry bread.

Fried Rice and Wheat

1 lb. ground beef
1 medium onion, chopped
3 cups rice
2 cups cooked wheat
Soy sauce

Brown ground beef in skillet with onion. Drain. Add rice and wheat and sauté until hot. Season with soy sauce. Serves 4.

1

Oriental Fried Rice with Wheat

2 tbsp. oil
3 eggs, beaten
Dash of salt
4 cups cooked rice, cooled
2 cups cooked wheat
2 tbsp. soy sauce
1 tsp. Accent
1 cup raw, shelled shrimp
1 tsp. cornstarch
1 cup ham, diced
¼ cup green onion, diced
½ cup frozen peas and carrots

In large skillet or wok, heat oil. Pour in eggs and salt and cook as an omelet; remove to cutting board and chop.

Heat more oil. Pour in rice, wheat, soy sauce, and Accent. Sauté until hot. Remove.

Heat more oil. Add shrimp and cornstarch. Sauté until shrimps are no longer pink, about 2 to 3 minutes. Remove.

Do not add more oil. Put ham, onion, peas and carrots into pan and sauté until hot. Combine all ingredients; stir and cook until hot. Serve with more soy sauce. (Good with egg foo yong, sweet and sour meatballs, egg rolls.) Serves 6.

Boston Baked Wheat

Bacon, as desired (4 slices to ½ lb.)
1 medium onion, chopped
5 cups cooked whole wheat
½ cup barbeque sauce
½ cup molasses
1 small can tomatoes, cut up
1 tsp. mustard
Salt and pepper to taste

Fry bacon until crisp; remove from pan and drain. Sauté onion in bacon grease until tender but not brown; remove from pan. Combine all ingredients except bacon in baking dish. Top with bacon. Bake ½ hour at 325 degrees F., or until hot. Serve with corn bread or hot dogs. Serves 4.

Chili Wheat

1 lb. ground beef
1 large onion, chopped
2 tsp. garlic powder
2 tbsp. chili powder
1 tsp. salt
1 large can whole tomatoes with liquid, cut up
1 tsp. Worcestershire sauce
1 tbsp. flour
2 beef boullion cubes
3 cups cooked wheat

Sauté meat and onions together until meat is browned. Add remaining ingredients except wheat. Bring to boil, reduce heat, and simmer gently for one hour. Add wheat and heat through. Serves 4.

Wheat, Barley, and Bean Stew

1 cup barley
½ cup small white beans
½ cup uncooked wheat
1 lb. ground beef
1 large onion, chopped
2 stalks celery, chopped
2 carrots, chopped
1 large can tomatoes, cut up
1 large can mushrooms, drained (optional)

Combine barley, beans, and wheat. Cover and soak overnight. Brown ground beef and onions. Add vegetables, barley, beans, and wheat, with water in which they have been soaking. Simmer gently 3 to 4 hours. Stir in mushrooms. (Also good when cooked in crockpot 8 hours. Eliminate soaking.) Serves 4 to 6.

Wheat Kernel Casserole

1 cup cooked wheat
1 lb. ground beef
1 large onion, chopped
3 tbsp. oil
1 cup celery, chopped
2 cups carrots, chopped
1 10 oz. can cream of mushroom soup
2 cups water
2 cups potato chips, crushed

Brown wheat, meat, and onion in oil. Drain. Add remaining ingredients except potato chips. Place 1 cup of potato chips in bottom of greased casserole. Place wheat mixture on top and sprinkle with remaining potato chips. Bake at 350 degrees F. for 45 minutes to 1 hour or until vegetables are done. Serves 4 to 6.

Wheat Treats

1. Soak uncooked wheat in cold water 24 to 48 hours, changing water once or twice during this time.
2. Drain wheat and let dry.
3. In heavy skillet, heat oil to 350 to 400 degrees F. Put a small amount of wheat directly into oil. Brown slightly, then remove with slotted spoon.
4. Drain on paper towels. Season with onion powder, garlic powder, seasoned salt, or whatever seasoning you prefer. Serve hot.

Whole Wheat Hot Cakes

1 cup boiling water
⅔ cup uncooked wheat
1 cup milk
1 tbsp. honey
3 eggs

Combine boiling water and wheat in pan and cover. Soak overnight. Drain and place wheat in blender with remaining ingredients. Blend on high speed until smooth. Bake on hot griddle. Makes about ten 4-inch hot cakes.

Cracked Wheat

Wheat grinders can grind wheat, but they don't seem to crack it as well as an ordinary blender does. If a grinder is used, you may wish to sift out the flour from the cracked wheat.

I have experimented with several blenders and discovered that not all blenders crack wheat satisfactorily. Some do not crack it at all, even when left on high speed, while others crack it much too fine. My blender is a Waring brand, and it seems to do a very good job. You may wish to experiment with your own blender. (Caution: Cracking whole grains may damage some blenders.)

To crack: Place ½ to 1 cup wheat or other grain in blender. Turn on at highest speed until each grain is cracked. Some grains will be cracked finer than others. If your blender jar is plastic, it will make a loud noise. Don't try it while the kids are down for their naps!

Cracked wheat can also be purchased at some health food stores and co-ops.

Multi-grain Cereal

1 cup cracked wheat
½ cup cracked rice
½ cup oats
¼ cup wheat bran or germ
¼ cup cornmeal
¼ cup flax seed

Combine all ingredients and store in an airtight container. To prepare, bring 2 cups water to boil. Stir in ½ cup cereal and ½ tsp. salt. Reduce heat and simmer gently for 15 minutes. This is a delicious hot cereal! Serves 2.

Note: If you do not have one of the above ingredients, leave it out! If you are fond of something in particular, add it! A few suggestions are coconut, raisins, cooked and roasted soy nuts, ground barley, sunflower seeds, sesame seeds.

Tip! Leftover cereal can be added to bread dough or used as a meat extender.

Chicken and Wheat Pilaf

2 tbsp. oil
2 cups cracked wheat
4 cups homemade chicken stock
Chicken, cooked and diced
Mixed vegetables (1 pkg. frozen or canned)

Heat oil in skillet. Add cracked wheat and sauté until all grains are coated. Pour in homemade stock. Cover and simmer for 15 minutes. Add chicken and vegetables. Cover and cook an additional five minutes. Serves 6.

Note: Boullion cubes or granules in water can be used for chicken stock, but the flavor won't be as good.

Tip! Homemade chicken stock is simple to make. After deboning the chicken, place all bones (and skin, if any) into pot. Cover with water and add about 2 tbsp. vinegar and 1 tbsp. salt. The vinegar will dissolve the calcium in the bones and bring it out into the stock, making it higher in calcium than milk. The salt brings out the flavor. The vinegar will also evaporate, leaving no vinegar taste. Simmer gently for 2 to 3 hours, or pressure cook for 30 minutes. Strain, and presto—delicious stock. You can also use the bones left after a fried chicken dinner. Simmering the stock will sterilize it.

Sesame and Wheat Pilaf

1 medium onion, chopped
¼ lb. mushrooms
¼ cup oil or bacon drippings
2 cups cracked wheat
½ cup sesame seeds, toasted
4 cups stock
1 clove garlic, minced
1 tbsp. parsley, chopped

Sauté the onion and mushrooms in oil. Add wheat and sesame seeds, and stir until all grains are coated with oil. Pour in stock, garlic, and parsley. Cover and simmer gently 15 to 20 minutes. Serves 4 to 6.

Note: A variety of pilafs can be made if you use your imagination. Cook wheat in any stock, tomato juice, or V-8 juice. Throw in leftover meat, vegetables, herbs, spices, mushrooms, diced green pepper, celery, or whatever you feel like adding. Be sure to sauté grain in 2 tbsp. oil before adding liquid. (See sprouted wheat section for more pilaf ideas.)

Basic Cracked Wheat Cereal

3 cups cold water
⅔ cup cracked wheat
1 tsp. salt

Combine all ingredients and bring to boil. Reduce heat and simmer for about 15 to 20 minutes. Serves 3 to 4.

Baked Chicken and Wheat

½ cup cracked wheat
1 10-oz. can cream of mushroom soup
1 cup chicken broth or stock
½ tsp. poultry seasoning
¼ tsp. sage
¼ cup margarine
1 pkg. chicken thighs
1 clove garlic, minced
½ cup chopped onion

Put wheat in casserole. In separate bowl combine soup, broth, poultry seasoning, and sage. Pour ½ of the soup mixture into casserole and mix with wheat. In skillet, melt margarine and brown chicken. Remove and arrange on top of wheat. Add garlic and onion to skillet and sauté until tender. Removed with slotted spoon and stir into remaining soup mixture. Add 1 tbsp. of the melted margarine to soup mixture, then pour over chicken. Bake at 350 degrees F. for one hour. Serves 4.

Mexican Casserole

1 lb. ground beef
1 large onion, chopped
Dash of salt
¾ cup uncooked cracked wheat
1 large can whole tomatoes, cut up
½ tsp. garlic powder
2 cups boiling water (use liquid from canned
    corn for part of water)
1 16-oz. can corn, drained
1 tsp. parsley flakes
2 cups grated cheese

Sauté ground beef, onion, and salt.
Place in casserole. Add remaining
ingredients, except cheese, and mix
well. Bake one hour at 325 degrees F.
When done, remove from oven and
stir in cheese. Serves 4 to 6.

Beef and Potato Casserole

1 lb. ground beef
1 large onion, chopped
1 clove garlic, crushed
1 tbsp. parsley flakes
1 tsp. celery flakes
Salt and pepper to taste
1 cup cracked wheat
2 medium potatoes, sliced
2 10-oz. cans tomato soup
Grated cheese

Sauté meat and onion with seasonings.
Add remaining ingredients, except
cheese. Bake at 350 degrees F. for
40 minutes, or until wheat is cooked
and potatoes are tender. Sprinkle cheese
on top during last 5 minutes. Serves 4 to 6.

Meatless Burritos

3 cups water
2 beef boullion cubes
⅓ cup cracked wheat
2 cups cooked pinto beans
1 medium onion, diced
¼ cup margarine
Salt to taste (1 tsp. or more)
2 tbsp. chili powder
⅓ cup enchilada sauce
1 cup grated cheese
3 medium potatoes, cooked and diced
12 flour tortillas
Oil for deep-fat frying

Combine water, boullion cubes, and
cracked wheat. Bring to boil, reduce heat,
and simmer gently 20 minutes or until
liquid is absorbed. Set aside to cool.
Meanwhile mash pinto beans and
combine with onion, margarine, salt,
chili powder, and enchilada sauce. Mix
well. Stir in grated cheese, potatoes, and
cracked wheat mixture. Place about
¼ cup or more in center of tortilla.
Wrap up; place in hot oil (375 degrees F.)
and cook until golden brown. Remove
and drain. Makes 12 burritos.
    Note: These measurements
can be adjusted to use more or less of the
ingredients you like.

Wheat Salad

5 cups cooled cracked wheat cereal
1/4 cup green pepper, diced
1/2 cup diced green onion
1 cup celery, diced fine
1 cup shrimp (or crab meat, chicken, turkey, or tuna)
1/2 to 1 cup mayonnaise
Salt to taste

Combine all ingredients and chill.
Serves 6 to 8.

Tip! Cooked, cooled cracked wheat (cooked as for cereal) is an excellent meat extender. Compare the cost of 1 pound of lean ground beef to 1 pound of wheat, and it's clear how economical wheat as a meat extender is. Wheat is also nourishing and satisfying. And most of all, your family won't be able to tell! (If they look, they can see it, but they can't taste it.) Simply combine equal parts cracked wheat with browned ground beef. When cooking the wheat, add some beef boullion cubes. Use the wheat/meat mixture in the following recipes, and use the mixture in any of your own favorite ground beef recipes.

Beef Pot Pie

1 medium onion, chopped
2 tbsp. oil or margarine
4 cups wheat/meat mixture (See p.7.)
2 1/2 cups gravy
1 cup cooked peas and carrots
2 tsp. Worcestershire sauce
Salt and pepper to taste
1 tbsp. dried parsley
Whole wheat pastry for 9-inch pie

Sauté onion in oil or margarine until tender. Combine all ingredients, except pastry, and mix well. Sprinkle with parsley. Pour into greased casserole dish. Top with pastry, pressing dough against rim of dish. Bake at 400 degrees F. for 35 minutes or until lightly browned. Serves 6.

Manicotti

16 manicotti shells (whole grain manicotti shells are available at health food stores and food co-ops.)
1/2 onion, chopped
3 cups wheat/meat mixture (See p.7.)
1 clove garlic, minced
1 cup whole wheat bread crumbs
1/2 lb. Mozzarella cheese, grated
1 tsp. salt
2 eggs, beaten slightly
2 to 3 cups spaghetti sauce

Cook manicotti shells in boiling water for 8 to 10 minutes or until tender, stirring occasionally. Drain and rinse in cold water. Meanwhile, heat oil and sauté onion; stir in wheat/meat mixture and sauté until heated through. Stir in remaining ingredients, except manicotti and spaghetti sauce. Mix well. Very carefully stuff manicotti shells with mixture. Lay in a single layer in a greased baking dish. Pour spaghetti sauce over the top. Bake at 350 degrees F. for 25 to 35 minutes. Serves 4.

Meatloaf Roll

4 cups wheat/meat mixture,
    unbrowned (See p. 7.)
2 eggs, slightly beaten
1 cup soft whole wheat bread crumbs
¼ cup catsup
½ tsp. salt
¼ tsp. oregano
1 tbsp. Worcestershire sauce
1 10-oz. pkg. frozen chopped broccoli, thawed
4 oz. Cheddar cheese, sliced

Mix together all ingredients, except broccoli and cheese. Pat into a 10x12-inch rectangle. Rinse broccoli under cold water and separate with fork. Spread broccoli over meat mixture, then top with cheese slices. Roll up, beginning at narrow end. (Place waxed paper or foil underneath, then lift as you roll.) Place in loaf pan and bake at 350 degrees F. for 1 to 1½ hours, or until done. Serves 6 to 8.

Sloppy Joes

1 lb. ground beef
1 medium onion, chopped
½ cup celery
1 cup V-8 juice or tomato juice
1 tsp. chili powder
⅓ cup cracked wheat
1 tbsp. Worcestershire sauce
Salt and pepper to taste

Sauté meat, onion, and celery until meat is browned. Add remaining ingredients and simmer 20 minutes, stirring occasionally. Serve over hamburger buns. Serves 4 to 6.

Tacos

1 medium onion, chopped
Oil
3 cups wheat/meat mixture (See p. 7.)
2 tbsp. chili powder
1 tsp. salt
½ tsp. cumin
1 tsp. garlic powder
Taco shells

In skillet sauté onion in oil until tender. Stir in remaining ingredients with ¾ cup water. Bring to boil, reduce heat, and simmer for 10 minutes. Serve in taco shells with chopped lettuce, grated cheese, tomato, chopped onion, and a dash of sour cream. Makes 8 tacos.

Enchilada Casserole

1 medium onion, chopped
Oil
3 cups wheat/meat mixture (See p. 7.)
1 8-oz. can enchilada sauce
1 10-oz. can cream of mushroom soup
1 pkg. flour tortillas, cut into 1-inch pieces
1 lb. grated Cheddar cheese
1 cup milk

Sauté onion in oil in skillet until tender. Stir in wheat/meat mixture, enchilada sauce, soup. Layer in a casserole dish: meat mixture, tortillas, and cheese. Pour milk over top. Bake at 350 degrees F. for 30 minutes. Serves 6.

Meaty Bean Burritos

2 cups wheat/meat mixture (See p. 7.)
¾ cup water
1 medium onion, chopped
2 tbsp. chili powder
1 tsp. salt
½ tsp. cumin
½ tsp. garlic powder
1 to 2 cups cooked pinto beans
½ cup grated Cheddar cheese
1 to 2 potatoes, cooked and diced
1 pkg. flour tortillas

Combine wheat/meat mixture, water, onion, chili powder, salt, cumin, and garlic powder in skillet and sauté until hot. Stir in pinto beans, cheese, and potatoes. Stir well. Spoon about ⅓ cup mixture on each tortilla. Roll up. Arrange on ungreased baking sheet. Cook uncovered at 350 degrees F. for about 20 minutes, or until hot. Garnish with shredded Monterey Jack cheese, sour cream, or enchilada sauce. Makes 8 burritos.

Meatballs

3 cups wheat/meat mixture, unbrowned (See p. 7.)
½ cup dry whole wheat bread crumbs
1 medium onion, chopped
1 egg
1 tsp. salt
½ tsp. Worcestershire sauce

Mix together all ingredients thoroughly. Shape into 1-inch balls. Brown in skillet on medium heat until browned on all sides and cooked to desired doneness. Serves 4.

Cheesy French Loaf

1 medium onion, chopped
2 tbsp. oil
2 cups wheat/meat mixture (See p. 7.)
1 10-oz can condensed Cheddar cheese soup
Salt, pepper
½ tsp. garlic powder
1 16-oz. loaf French bread

Sauté onion in oil in skillet. Stir in wheat/meat mixture, soup, salt, pepper, and garlic powder. Set aside. With sharp knife, cut off top of French loaf. Gently pull out soft bread, leaving shell. Tear bread into 1-inch pieces and stir into wheat/meat mixture. Stir well. Stuff bread shell and replace top. Bake at 350 degrees F. for 15 minutes or until thoroughly heated. Serves 4.

Note: To keep bread from becoming too dried out during baking, rub with margarine before baking.

Sprouted Wheat

Sprouting is a simple process and greatly increases the nutritional value of grains, beans, and seeds. Not only do the seeds and grains increase in food value, but they also develop nutrients that were not present before in measurable quantities, such as vitamin C. In addition, the starch changes to sugar in grains, making them easier to digest, and a delight to eat raw.

Add sprouts to salads, soups, casseroles, and sandwiches. Cook them with vegetables or eggs, or dry them and grind them into flour. Use them in breads. Sprouts will quicken the leavening action of leavened breads, and help unleavened bread to rise. When fresh sprouts are included in breads, they usually rise in about half the time it normally takes.

To sprout: A commercial sprouter is a simple and convenient way to sprout, and as many as four or more different grains can be sprouted at once. However, sprouting can be done in a glass jar: Put 1 tbsp. wheat (or other grain or seed) in a pint jar or 2 tbsp. in a quart jar. Fill half full with warm water and let soak overnight. Place a piece of nylon netting or cheesecloth over the top of the jar and secure it with a rubber band or jar ring. Next morning, drain off the water. (Save it—it is chock full of vitamins and minerals. Use it in your cooking or baking, or feed it to your plants.) Fill the jar with warm water again and pour off. Turn jar upside down at an angle so that the water can drain off during the day. That evening, rinse and drain seeds again. Do this night and morning until they are sprouted. Wheat takes about 2 days. The sprouts are ready when the sprout part is the same length as the wheat berry. Other seeds and grains take 2 to 4 days.

Remember: Sprouted wheat multiplies the food value of wheat ten times.

Wheat Sprout Salad

2 cups fresh wheat sprouts
½ cup grated carrot
1 small onion, minced
3 tbsp. oil
1 tbsp. cider vinegar or lemon juice
Paprika
Sesame seeds

Combine all ingredients and chill. Serves 4.

Sprouted Wheat Balls
(A delicious snack or hors d'oeuvre)

½ cup cream cheese
1 cup fresh wheat sprouts
1 cup chopped nuts
1 cup chopped raisins
Sesame seeds

Combine cream cheese, sprouts, nuts, and raisins. Mix thoroughly. Roll into balls, then roll in sesame seeds. Chill.

Wheat Sprout "Meatballs"

2 cups sprouts
1 medium onion
1 cup nuts (optional)
2 cups whole wheat bread crumbs
1 tsp. salt
1 cup milk
2 tsp. oil
2 beaten eggs

Put sprouts, onion, and nuts through a food grinder with fine blade, or grind in a food processor. Add remaining ingredients. Shape into balls, walnut size. Brown in oil in skillet until heated through. Serves 4.

Wheat Sprout Candy

½ cup fresh wheat sprouts
½ cup nuts
½ cup coconut
½ cup raisins
Peanut butter (if needed)
Honey (if needed)

Grind all ingredients except peanut butter and honey in food grinder with a fine blade. Roll into marble-size balls. Add a little peanut butter and honey, if necessary, to make balls hold together.

Wheat Sprout Pancakes

1 cup fresh wheat sprouts, dried
1½ cups water
2 cups whole wheat flour
1 tsp. salt
3 tsp. baking powder
¼ cup oil
1¼ cups milk

Crack sprouted wheat in blender. Combine with water and soak overnight. Next morning drain and, combine with remaining ingredients and blend in blender until smooth. Fry on hot griddle. Serves 6.

Sprout Casserole

2 tbsp. oil
2 tbsp. whole wheat flour
2 cups milk
1 tbsp. Worcestershire sauce
1 tsp. salt
1 cup cheese, diced
¼ cup onion, minced
¼ cup celery, chopped
2 cups fresh wheat sprouts
2 cups cooked egg noodles (Whole grain
     noodles are available in health food
     stores or food co-ops.)
Paprika
Butter

Heat oil and blend in flour. Gradually stir in milk and cook until thick, stirring constantly. Add Worcestershire sauce, salt, and cheese; add all remaining ingredients, except paprika. Heat until cheese melts slightly. Pour into greased casserole. Sprinkle with paprika and dot with butter. Bake at 350 degrees F. for 30 minutes or until hot. Serves 6.

Harvest Sprout Casserole

½ onion, chopped
1 tbsp. oil
1½ cups roast beef or pork, diced
1 cup beef broth
1 cup canned tomatoes
1 tbsp. chili powder
1 cup sprouted wheat
Salt and pepper to taste
1 tbsp. whole wheat flour
¼ cup water

Cook onion in oil until tender. Add the beef or pork, broth, tomatoes, chili powder, sprouts, and salt and pepper. Simmer for about 30 minutes. Combine flour and water and add to sauce to thicken. Simmer a few minutes. Pour over hot cooked rice or noodles. Serves 4.

Wheat Sprout Pilaf

2 tbsp. oil
2 cups whole or cracked wheat sprouts
1 large carrot, chopped
1 large onion, chopped
½ cup celery, chopped
3 cups beef stock
Dash of Worcestershire sauce

Heat oil in skillet and stir in wheat sprouts. Stir until all grains are coated. Add carrot and onion, then celery. Sauté 2 minutes. Stir in beef stock, reduce heat, and simmer for 45 minutes. Stir in a dash of Worcestershire sauce before serving.

Ground Wheat (Flour)

Wheat flour, fresh from a stone grinder as it is ground, is the most desirable flour to use. Grain that is stone-ground is more desirable because the heat generated in metal grinders destroys many nutrients. However, grinding your own wheat is not always possible. Wheat grinders are expensive to buy, and often not available for borrowing either. But that should not stop anyone from cooking with whole wheat flour. Stone-ground whole wheat flour is available at most food co-ops and health food stores. Most grocery stores also carry whole wheat flour. While flour bought in the stores is not of the superior quality that fresh, stone-ground flour is, nevertheless it contains many nutrients, roughage, protein, and essential oils that white flour, even "enriched" white flour, does not. Now that you know how to use wheat without grinding it (whole, sprouted, and cracked), go ahead and buy the flour. When you and your family discover how delicious it is, perhaps purchase of a wheat grinder can be planned.

I use whole wheat flour for everything—cooking, baking, pie crusts, to flour chicken before frying, to thicken gravies—in everything! I don't stop to analyze whether whole wheat flour is going to work or not, I just use it. When I see a recipe that calls for flour, I automatically think of whole wheat flour without giving it a second thought. Usually I reduce the quantity to ⅞ cup, or 1 cup less 2 tbsp. But in cakes, where I automatically use honey instead of sugar, reducing the flour is not necessary. The honey adds enough liquid to make up for using whole grain flour.

I do have a couple of exceptions. Muffins and rolls can be made with whole wheat flour, but that doesn't seem to be the case with biscuits. To make a light, fluffy biscuit, I find that I need to use *half* white flour. And when making bread, I usually use white flour while kneading to prevent dough from sticking.

Note: There *is* a difference between bread flour and pastry flour, an important difference. Do not use *bread flour* in cakes and pies, and do not use *pastry flour* in breads.

BREADS

Tips for making yeast breads:

1. When combining liquid and initial addition of flour, beat with electric mixer for at least 7 minutes. A lot of mixing and kneading are necessary for light, delicious bread.

2. Use white flour when kneading bread; it prevents sticking more effectively.

3. Bread should be kneaded for no less than 10 minutes before allowing to rise.

4. Use 1-pound loaf pans instead of 1½-pound loaf pans, which are commonly used for bread. The bottom should measure 4½ by 8½ inches.

5. A 100-degree F. temperature is ideal for rising bread. Use your dehydrator if you have one. If not, turn the oven on for about a minute, then shut off, place bread in oven, and close door. Letting dough rise twice is not necessary unless you prefer it. Dough may be molded into pans and rise once.

6. While allowing bread to rise in pans, do not let it over-rise. This is a common error. Allow bread to rise for only 20 minutes. Bread will continue to rise during the baking. (If bread has risen beautifully then fallen during the baking, or if there are huge air holes in your bread, you have probably let it over-rise the final time.)

7. Preheating the oven is not necessary. When bread is ready for baking, place loaves in oven (if they are not already there) and turn the oven to 350 degrees F. Begin timing when oven reaches 350 degrees F.

8. For superior texture, mix in about ⅓ cup *whey* (available at health food stores and food co-ops) for every 4 loaves of bread. Read the labels on bread in the grocery store, and you'll see that most bakeries have discovered this secret.

Basic Whole Wheat Bread

4½ cups warm water
1 cup honey
4 tbsp. yeast
½ cup oil
6 cups whole wheat flour
1½ tsp. salt
4½ cups whole wheat flour

Combine water, honey, and yeast; let sit 5 minutes or longer. Then add oil, 6 cups flour, and salt. Beat with electric mixer for 7 minutes. Add remaining flour. Stir, then turn onto floured board and knead for at least 10 minutes. Add more flour as needed to prevent sticking. Mold into bread pans. Let rise 20 minutes. Bake at 350 degrees F. for 35 minutes or until golden brown. Makes 4 loaves.

Cinnamon Rolls

Cut Basic Whole Wheat Bread recipe in half. Add 1 or 2 eggs when you add oil. Proceed as directed, adding more flour as necessary. Roll out into rectangle. Spread with softened margarine, sprinkle with cinnamon and sugar. Roll up, cut into pieces about 2 inches thick. Place pieces, just barely touching, on cookie sheet and allow rolls to rise 15 minutes. Bake at 350 degrees F. for about 20 minutes or until golden brown.

Cinnamon Bread

Prepare basic recipe as directed. Roll out into four rectangles. Spread with softened margarine, cinnamon, and sugar. Roll up and place in loaf pan. Let rise 20 minutes, and bake at 350 degrees F. for 35 minutes.

Scones

After Basic Whole Wheat Bread has risen punch down and roll out about 1 inch thick or less. Heat oil in skillet. Cut bread dough into squares or rectangular shapes. Place in hot oil. Turn when browned on one side. Serve with honey, jam, syrup, or honey butter.

Pizza Dough

Use bread dough for one loaf of bread; divide in half and spread thin on two large pizza pans. Top with spaghetti sauce, cheese, and meat if desired. Bake at 400 degrees F. for 10 to 15 minutes.

Tip! Spread dough with light coat of oil before topping with other ingredients to keep dough crispy.

Dinner Rolls

Use the equivalent of one or two loaves of bread dough.

Cloverleaf Rolls: Roll dough into 1-inch balls. Place three balls for each muffin in greased tins. Brush with melted margarine.

Four-leaf Clovers: Roll dough into 2-inch balls. Place in greased muffin tins. With scissors, cut into halves, then fourths. Brush with melted margarine.

Parkerhouse Rolls: Roll dough out to about ½ to ¾ inch thick. Cut into 3-inch rounds. Brush with melted margarine; fold in half. Place on baking sheet.

Basic Rolls: Roll dough into 2- or 3-inch balls. Brush palms of hands with melted margarine, then roll balls to lightly coat with margarine. Place just barely touching in greased baking pan.

Let dough rise for about 15 minutes, then bake at 350 degrees F. for 20 minutes, or until lightly browned.

Bread Sticks

Follow recipe for whole wheat bread and allow bread to rise once. Break off small pieces and roll into long narrow sticks, about ½ inch thick and 4 to 6 inches long. Roll in melted margarine, then in garlic, Parmesan cheese, and/or parsley flakes. (If you choose more than one ingredient, mix together). Let rise for about 15 minutes, then bake at 350 degrees F. for 10 to 15 minutes, or until browned. Bake longer for crispier sticks.

Extra-Good Whole Wheat Bread

½ cup water
2 tbsp. yeast
1 tsp. sugar
⅓ cup honey
1 tbsp. salt
3 eggs
4 cups milk
¼ cup melted margarine
10 cups whole wheat flour
¼ tsp. baking soda

Stir together water, yeast, and sugar, and let sit 5 minutes or longer. In larger bowl, combine honey, salt, eggs, melted margarine, and 5 cups whole wheat flour. Add yeast mixture to flour-and-egg mixture. Beat with electric mixer for 10 minutes. Stir in 5 cups more flour and baking soda. Knead well for 10 minutes, adding more flour as needed to prevent sticking. Mold into 4 baking pans. Let rise for 20 minutes. Bake at 350 degrees F. for 35 minutes. Makes 4 loaves.

Another Whole Wheat Bread Recipe

2 tbsp. yeast
½ cup warm water
1 tsp. sugar
6 eggs
3 cups milk, scalded and cooled
½ cup honey
1 cup oil
1 tbsp. salt
Whole wheat flour
1 tbsp. salt

Dissolve yeast in warm water; add sugar. Set aside. Beat eggs. Add cooled milk, honey, oil, then yeast mixture. Add salt and enough flour to make a stiff batter (dough will be too soft to handle). Let rise. Stir down and pour into 3 greased bread pans. Start baking at 400 degrees F., then immediately reduce heat to 350 degrees F. for 30 to 45 minutes, or until done. Makes 3 loaves.

Bran Muffins

1½ cups unprocessed bran
¾ cup milk
1 cup whole wheat flour
1 tsp. baking soda
1 egg, well beaten
½ cup honey or light molasses
¼ cup oil

Soften bran in milk for a few minutes. Stir together flour and baking soda. Add remaining ingredients; stir only enough to barely blend. Bake in greased muffin tins at 400 degrees F. for 20 to 30 minutes. Makes about 12.

Biscuits

1 tbsp. baking powder
1 cup whole wheat pastry flour
¾ cup unbleached white flour
¾ tsp. salt
⅓ cup shortening
¾ cup milk

Combine baking powder, flours, and salt. Cut in shortening with pastry blender or 2 knives, until shortening pieces are the size of tiny peas. Stir in milk, stirring only 10 times. Turn onto floured board and knead 8 or 10 times. Pat to about 1 inch thick. Cut with biscuit cutter. Bake at 450 degrees F. for 10 minutes, or until golden brown. Makes 1 dozen biscuits.

Note: You may use ½ cup water blended with ⅓ cup yogurt in place of ¾ cup milk.

Dumplings No. 1

Follow recipe for biscuits, reducing margarine to ¼ cup. Stir as little as possible; do not knead. Drop by teaspoonfuls onto hot boiling stew on top of meat or vegetables. Cook uncovered for about 10 minutes, then cook covered for an additional 10 minutes. *Note:* For herb dumplings, stir ½ tsp. herbs and 1 tbsp. parsley flakes into flour before adding liquid.

Dumplings No. 2

1 cup whole wheat flour
1 egg
⅓ cup water
3 tsp. baking powder
½ tsp. salt

Combine all ingredients. Drop onto hot stew or soup. Cover and cook for 15 minutes. Don't peek.

Cheese-Filled Rolls

1 8-oz. pkg. cream cheese
¼ cup sugar
3 tbsp. whole wheat flour
1 egg yolk
½ tsp. grated lemon peel
1 tbsp. lemon juice
Bread dough for one loaf of bread
½ cup jam
Chopped nuts

Beat cream cheese and sugar until light and fluffy. Stir in flour, egg yolk, lemon peel, and lemon juice. Roll bread dough into a 15-inch square. Cut into twenty-five 3-inch squares. Place on greased cookie sheets. Spoon about 1 tbsp. cream cheese mixture into center of each square. Bring all four corners up, overlapping slightly, and pinch together. Let rise for about 15 minutes. Bake at 350 degrees F. for about 12 minutes or until golden brown. Heat jam until melted. Spoon over the top of rolls, then sprinkle with nuts. Makes 25.

Whole Wheat Crackers

½ cup milk
1 tbsp. vinegar
1¾ cups whole wheat flour
¼ tsp. soda
½ cup margarine
1 tbsp. sugar

Combine milk and vinegar and set aside. Combine remaining ingredients in bowl and knead until it resembles coarse meal. Add milk mixture. Turn onto floured board and knead briefly; roll out thin, about ¼ inch thick. Place on cookie sheet and prick with fork. Bake at 375 degrees F. for 5 to 10 minutes.

Sesame Crackers

3 cups whole wheat flour
1 cup cornmeal
1 tsp. salt
¾ cup oil
½ cup water
Sesame seeds
Garlic powder

Mix flour, cornmeal, and salt together. Stir in oil. Add water gradually until dough is soft, but holds together. Do not knead too much. Roll out thin. Sprinkle with seeds and garlic. Cut into squares. Bake at 375 degrees F. for 20 to 30 minutes.

Chappati

2 cups whole wheat flour
½ tsp. salt
¾ to 1 cup water

Blend flour and salt. Stir in just enough water to make a stiff dough. Knead on floured board until smooth and elastic. Break off dough and form into 1-inch balls. Roll very thin, into 8-inch rounds. Bake on hot griddle sprinkled with salt to prevent sticking, or griddle may be lightly greased. Serve warm with honey butter. Serves 6.

Oatmeal Muffins

1 cup rolled oats
⅔ cup milk
1 egg
½ cup oil
1 cup whole wheat flour
¼ cup sugar
3 tsp. baking powder
1 tsp. baking soda
1 tsp. salt

Heat oven to 400 degrees F. Grease bottom of 12 muffin tins. Soften oats in milk a few minutes. Beat egg, stir in oil. Add milk and oats, then remaining ingredients. Stir until just barely mixed. Bake for 20 minutes. Makes about 12.

Wheat and Soy Pancake Mix

4 cups whole wheat flour
4 cups soy flour
½ tsp. baking powder
1 tsp. salt
3 tbsp. sugar

Mix all ingredients together and store in container with tight-fitting lid. To make pancakes, combine 1 cup mix, 1 cup plus 1 tbsp. water or milk, 1 egg, and 1 tbsp. oil. Mix together and bake on hot griddle. Serves 2 to 3.

Whole Wheat Waffles

3 eggs
2 cups water
½ cup oil
½ tsp. salt
1 tbsp. baking powder
2 cups whole wheat flour

In two medium bowls, separate eggs. With electric mixer, beat whites until stiff peaks form. Set aside. With same beaters (no need to wash off), beat together water, egg yolks, and oil. Beat in salt, baking powder, and flour. Spread egg whites over mixture, then gently fold in. Bake on hot waffle iron. Leftover waffles may be stored in freezer and heated in toaster. Serves 3 to 4.

Whole Wheat Pancakes

1¼ cups water
2 eggs
1 tbsp. oil
1 cup whole wheat flour
2 tsp. baking powder
½ tsp. salt.

Beat water, eggs, and oil together. Stir in flour, baking powder, and salt. Stir until just barely mixed. Fry on hot griddle. This will satisfy two hearty appetites.
     Note: For lighter pancakes, separate eggs, beat whites until stiff; fold in last of all.

Soy Pancakes

Follow above recipe, substituting ½ cup soy flour for ½ cup of the whole wheat flour. These are light, delicious pancakes. Serve them to a family who think they don't like whole grain pancakes. These look almost as though they were made with regular white flour.

Whole Wheat Noodles

1 cup flour
1 egg
1 tbsp. milk or water

Combine all ingredients and roll out thin, using flour on bread board as needed. Cut into strips as thin as desired. Cook immediately, or dry in dehydrator or warm oven. Store.

DESSERTS

Whole grain desserts are great to serve to your family. They are delicious to eat, contain many vitamins and minerals, and are not just "empty" calories, like refined sweets.

When I make cookies from other recipes, I usually substitute whole wheat flour for white, sometimes reducing the amount slightly. In almost every dessert recipe I have found, the sugar or honey can be reduced by as much as one-half. I serve cookies, cake, and other desserts to my friends and family, and everyone agrees that they are good and sweet.

When I make cakes or bar cookies or fruit crisps, I usually substitute honey for sugar. In fact, I use honey whenever I can—that is, whenever honey will not change the texture too much. Also, when I make cakes, I usually use one more egg than the original recipe calls for, separate the eggs, whip the whites to a soft peak, and fold the whites in last of all. And I increase the leavening by one-half to one teaspoon in many recipes.

Cakes

Tip! Cakes do not need egg yolks, and can have 2, 3, or even 4 egg whites in them. If you have egg whites left over from another recipe such as vanilla pudding or egg nog, this is a good way to use them up. Always whip them until soft peaks form, and then fold into the batter just before pouring it into cake pans.

Sweet Potato Cake

2 cups whole wheat pastry flour
1 ⅓ cups honey or sugar
2 tsp. baking soda
1 tsp. baking powder
2 tsp. cinnamon
1 tsp. pumpkin pie spice
½ tsp. salt
1 tsp. vanilla
4 eggs, separated
1 cup oil
2 cups sweet potatoes, cooked and mashed
1 cup chopped nuts (optional)

Beat together all ingredients except egg whites. Beat egg whites until stiff, and spread over cake batter. Gently fold in with large spoon. Pour into well-greased and floured fluted cake pan. Bake at 350 degrees F. until done, about 40 minutes. Frost with glaze or thin frosting, if desired.

Pineapple Cake

3 eggs, separated
1 ½ cups sugar or honey
2 cups whole wheat pastry flour
2 tsp. baking soda
1 20-oz. can undrained pineapple chunks
1 tsp. vanilla
1 cup chopped nuts

Beat egg whites until soft peaks form; set aside. In large bowl, combine remaining ingredients and mix well. Spread egg whites over the top and gently fold in. Pour into oiled and floured 9x13-inch pan. Bake at 350 degrees F. for 35 to 40 minutes. Frost with cream cheese frosting while cake is still warm.

Cream Cheese Frosting

Combine one 8-oz. pkg. cream cheese and ½ stick (¼ cup) butter. Beat well. Add 1¾ cups powdered sugar and 1 tsp. vanilla. Beat until smooth.

Orange Bundt Cake

2½ cups whole wheat pastry flour 1¼ cups sugar 2 tsp. baking soda ¾ tsp. salt 1½ cups water ½ cup margarine ¼ cup shortening 3 eggs, separated 1 tbsp. orange peel 2 tsp. vanilla	Beat all ingredients together until well mixed. Pour into greased and floured fluted cake pan. Bake at 350 degrees F. for 55 to 60 minutes or until done. Frost, if desired, when cool.

Carrot Cake

2 cups grated carrots 2 cups whole wheat pastry flour 1 10-oz. can diced pineapple, drained 1 cup currants or raisins, chopped 1 cup walnuts, chopped 4 eggs, beaten ⅓ cup honey ⅓ cup oil 1 tsp. cinnamon 1 tsp. salt ½ tsp. nutmeg	Mix all ingredients together well. Pour into oiled and floured 9x13-inch pan. Bake one hour at 350 degrees F. Frost with cream cheese frosting (p. 20) when cool.

Chocolate Mayonnaise Cake

2 cups whole wheat pastry flour
2 tsp. baking soda
6 level tbsp. cocoa, carob, or combination
    of both
Dash of salt
1 cup honey
1 cup mayonnaise
¾ cup cold water
1 tsp. vanilla

Combine dry ingredients. Add remaining ingredients and mix well. Beat until smooth. Bake at 350 degrees F. in greased and floured pan(s) until done.

muffin tins	20 minutes
8x8-inch pan	30 to 35 minutes
round cake pan	30 to 35 minutes
9x13-inch pan	35 to 40 minutes

For extra good texture, add one egg yolk and one stiffly beaten egg white.

Pound Cake

1 cup margarine	Cream margarine until light and fluffy.
1⅓ cups sugar	Gradually beat in sugar. Add egg yolks
5 eggs, separated	one at a time, beating well after each
1¾ cups whole wheat pastry flour	addition. Stir flour and mace into batter.
1 tsp. mace	Whip whites until soft peaks form.
	Fold into batter (batter will be stiff). Pour
	into greased fluted cake pan. Bake at
	350 degrees F. for 45 minutes or until golden
	brown and done.

Company Chocolate Cake

2 cups whole wheat pastry flour
1¼ cups honey or sugar
2 tsp. baking powder
1 tsp. baking soda
1 tsp. salt
1 cup water
½ cup oil
1 tsp. vanilla
6 tbsp. cocoa, carob, or a combination
    of both
3 eggs, separated

Beat together until smooth all ingredients except egg whites. Beat egg whites to form soft peaks. Spread over batter; gently fold in. Bake at 350 degrees F.

muffin tins	20 minutes
8x8-inch pan	30 to 35 minutes
round pans	30 to 35 minutes
9x13-inch pan	35 to 40 minutes

Tip! Carob can be used as a substitute for chocolate. It is dark brown like cocoa, but unlike cocoa, it contains no caffeine, has fewer calories, and costs less. Unfortunately it does not taste like cocoa, and many people do not care for the taste. However by using half carob and half cocoa powder in your recipes, no one will be able to taste the carob because cocoa has such a strong flavor. It is a good way to reduce the amount of chocolate your family eats and save money. They will probably never know the difference.

Cookies

Sugar Cookies

½ lb. margarine (two sticks)	Beat together margarine, eggs, sugar,
3 eggs	vanilla, and sour cream until light and
2 cups sugar	fluffy. Add baking powder and flour.
2 tsp. vanilla	Refrigerate several hours or overnight.
8-oz. carton sour cream	Roll out thin and cut with cookie cutter.
2 tsp. baking powder	Bake on ungreased cookie sheet at
3 cups whole wheat flour	375 degrees F. for about 8 to 10 minutes,
2 cups white flour	until lightly browned. Cool on wire
	rack. Makes 5 dozen 4-inch cookies.

Chocolate Drop Cookies

1 cup sugar
½ cup margarine
1 egg
1 tsp. molasses
1 tsp. vanilla
2 tbsp. oil
6 tbsp. cocoa or carob or combination of both
1½ cups whole wheat flour
½ tsp. baking soda
½ tsp. baking powder
½ tsp. salt

Beat together sugar, margarine, egg, molasses, vanilla, and oil until light and fluffy. Beat in remaining ingredients. Drop by tablespoons onto greased cookie sheet. Bake at 350 degrees F. for 10 to 15 minutes or until barely browned on bottom. Cool on wire rack. Makes 2 dozen large cookies.

Chocolate Chip Cookies

⅓ cup granulated sugar
⅓ cup brown sugar
⅔ cup shortening (part may be margarine)
1 egg
1 tsp. vanilla
1½ cups whole wheat flour
½ tsp. baking soda
½ tsp. salt
1 cup chocolate chips

Beat together sugars, shortening, egg, and vanilla. Stir in remaining ingredients. Add 1 or 2 tbsp. more flour if needed. Drop by teaspoonfuls onto greased cookie sheet. Bake at 350 degrees F. until lightly browned, about 10 minutes. Cool on wire rack. (Cookies will continue to bake as they are cooling.) Makes 2 dozen large cookies.

Sweet Potato and Molasses Cookies

½ cup margarine or butter
½ cup sugar
1 egg
½ cup molasses
1 cup raw sweet potato, peeled and grated
1¾ cups whole wheat pastry flour
½ tsp. salt
½ tsp. baking soda
½ tsp. baking powder
½ tsp. cinnamon
½ tsp. ginger
¼ cup milk

Cream together butter and sugar. Add egg and beat thoroughly. Blend in molasses and sweet potato. Stir in flour and remaining dry ingredients. Then add milk. Drop onto a greased cookie sheet by teaspoonfuls. Bake at 375 degrees F. for 12 to 15 minutes, until browned. Cool on wire rack. Makes 3 dozen cookies.

Molasses Cookies

¼ cup margarine
¼ cup blackstrap molasses
1 egg
½ cup sugar
1 cup whole wheat pastry flour
¼ tsp. salt
¼ tsp. cloves
¼ tsp. cinnamon
½ cup chopped walnuts (optional)

Cream margarine and molasses. Beat in egg, then sugar. Beat in remaining ingredients. Drop by teaspoonfuls onto greased cookie sheet. Bake at 375 degrees F. for 10 to 15 minutes. Cool on wire rack. Makes 2 dozen cookies.

Chocolate Chip-Peanut Butter Brownies

½ cup creamy peanut butter
⅓ cup margarine
⅓ cup sugar
⅓ cup brown sugar
2 eggs
1 tsp. vanilla
1 cup whole wheat flour
1 tsp. baking powder
¼ tsp. salt
1 6-oz. pkg. chocolate chips

Cream together peanut butter, margarine, and sugars until light and fluffy. Beat in eggs and vanilla. Combine dry ingredients in separate bowl and add to creamed mixture, stirring well. Stir in chocolate chips. Pour into well-buttered, 8-inch square baking pan. Bake at 350 degrees F. for 35 minutes. Do not overbake. Cool in pan, then cut into bars. Makes 9 bars.

Peach Cobbler

1 tbsp. baking powder
½ cup sugar
1 cup whole wheat pastry flour
¾ cup white flour
¾ tsp. salt
⅓ cup shortening
¾ cup milk or water
4 pints canned peaches, drained (reserve
        1 cup of liquid)
¼ cup whole wheat flour
1 tsp. cinnamon

Combine baking powder, sugar, flours, and salt; cut in shortening with pastry cutter or two knives. Pour in liquid and stir till barely mixed. Place on board and knead 15 times. Pat out till ½ inch thick. In saucepan combine 1 cup reserved peach juice, ¼ cup flour, and cinnamon. Bring to boil and simmer 1 to 2 minutes. Pour peaches into baking dish. Pour peach juice on top. Cut biscuits with cutter into 3-inch rounds and place on top. Bake at 350 degrees F. for 30 minutes or longer, until biscuits are not doughy on underside and peaches are heated through.

Baked Fruit and Streusel

Streusel topping:
   ½ cup dried whole wheat bread crumbs
   ½ cup whole wheat flour
   ½ cup margarine
   ½ cup sugar
   1½ tsp. cinnamon
Fruit:
   2 16-oz. cans sliced peaches
   1 39-oz. can sliced pears
   3 tbsp. whole wheat flour
   ½ tsp. cinnamon

Mix ingredients for streusel topping and set aside. Drain syrup from fruit, reserving ⅓ cup. Place peaches and pears in buttered baking dish. Combine syrup, 3 tbsp. flour, and cinnamon in saucepan. Cook over medium heat until thickened. Pour over fruit. Top with streusel topping. Bake at 400 degrees for 20 to 30 minutes or until hot. Serve with ice cream or whipped topping. Serves 6.

Note: 1 quart home-canned peaches and 1 quart home-canned pears may be substituted for store-bought fruit.

Banana Nut Bread

2½ cups whole wheat flour
4 tsp. baking powder
1 tsp. salt
1 cup chopped nuts
2 tbsp. oil
1 cup honey
¼ cup milk or water
1 egg
1 cup bananas, mashed

Combine dry ingredients and mix well. Stir in nuts. Add remaining ingredients, stirring no more than 40 strokes. Bake at 350 degrees F. in large greased loaf pan (1½-lb.) for 45 minutes or until done.

Whole Wheat Pastry

½ cup margarine
½ cup sugar
2 cups whole wheat pastry flour
1 tsp. cinnamon
⅛ tsp. salt

Mix all ingredients together with electric mixer until crumbly. Add just enough *cold* water to make mixture hold together, about 2 or 3 tablespoons. Roll between 2 pieces of waxed paper. Makes one bottom and one top crust.

Apple Crisp

4 cups apples, peeled and sliced
½ cup honey
½ cup whole wheat flour
½ cup rolled oats, uncooked
½ tsp. cinnamon
¼ tsp. nutmeg
⅓ cup margarine

Arrange apples in a greased 8-inch square pan or baking dish. Mix together remaining ingredients. Spread over apples. Bake at 350 degrees F. for 30 minutes. Serve warm or cold. Serves 9.

OATS

Oats are a natural, whole grain. They contain significant amounts of iron, phosphorus, potassium, and other nutrients. Fairly fine oat flour can be made by whirling rolled oats in the blender. A fine flour can be made by grinding them in a wheat grinder.

Of course, oats added to meatloaf has long been a favorite main dish. Delicious hamburgers can be made by omitting the egg in the meatloaf recipe and reducing the liquid.

Oatmeal cookies are a time-tested favorite. But there are many more desserts you can make from oats than oatmeal cookies. Granola is a real hit. It makes a delicious breakfast cereal served cold with milk. Many, many desserts can also be made from granola. With all the seeds, wheat germ, non-instant milk, and other good things, granola is super-nutritious!

Granola

2½ cups old-fashioned or regular rolled oats
½ cup shredded coconut
½ cup sesame seeds
½ cup sunflower seeds
½ cup wheat germ or bran
½ cup soy or whole wheat flour
½ cup non-instant powdered milk
½ cup chopped nuts (optional)
½ cup oil
½ cup honey

Combine all ingredients except oil and honey; mix well. In separate bowl, stir together honey and oil. Pour over oat mixture and blend well. Spread in one or two large oblong cake pans or cookie sheets. Bake at 300 degrees F. for 20 minutes or more until golden brown. Stir often and watch it carefully. It can burn easily! Makes about 6 cups.

Cereal Balls

Grind granola in blender. Stir in a little peanut butter and honey. Add a few drops of milk, if necessary. Roll into balls; refrigerate.

Granola Peanut Crunch Bars

⅔ cup honey
⅓ cup peanut butter
½ tsp. vanilla
2 cups granola
1 cup peanuts or soy nuts

Stir honey over medium heat until it boils. Stir in peanut butter and vanilla. Mix granola and peanuts together. Pour honey mixture over granola mixture. Pat into 8-inch square greased pan. Cool. Cut into bars. Makes 9 bars.

Granola Macaroon Bars

2 cups rolled oats
2 cups granola
⅔ cup melted butter or margarine
½ cup honey
¼ tsp. salt
2 tsp. vanilla

Combine all ingredients. Pour into oiled 9x13-inch pan. Bake at 325 degrees F. for about 20 minutes or until lightly browned and firm. Frost when cool, if desired. Makes 18 bars.

Granola Mallow Bars

1 10-oz. pkg. marshmallows
¼ cup margarine
½ cup peanut butter
4 cups granola

Melt marshmallows, margarine, and peanut butter. Stir in granola. Spread in 9x13-inch buttered pan. Cool, then cut into bars. Makes 18 bars.
    Note: Bars can also be rolled into logs.

Granola Apple Crisp

4 cups apples, peeled and sliced
½ cup margarine
⅓ cup honey
1½ cups granola
½ cup whole wheat flour
¼ tsp. cinnamon

Place apples in a greased 8-inch square pan. In saucepan, heat margarine until melted. Remove from heat, and blend in honey. Stir in remaining ingredients. Pour (or spread) over apples. Bake at 350 degrees F. for 35 minutes. Serves 9.

Oatmeal Crisps

⅔ cup margarine
1¾ cups brown sugar
1 tsp. baking powder
⅛ tsp. salt
1 tsp. vanilla
1 egg, beaten
2 tbsp. whole wheat flour
2½ cups rolled oats

Cream margarine and brown sugar until light and creamy. Mix in the rest of the ingredients and drop by teaspoonfuls 2 inches apart onto a greased cookie sheet. Bake at 350 degrees F. for about 10 minutes or until golden brown. Let cool before removing from pan. Let stand a couple of hours before storing in jar. Makes 2 dozen.

Oatmeal Macaroons

4 cups rolled oats
⅔ cup honey
4 tsp. grated orange rind
½ tsp. salt
⅔ cup oil
2 eggs, beaten
½ cup chopped nuts

Combine oats, honey, orange rind, and salt. Add oil, eggs, and nuts. Chill several hours. Drop onto cookie sheet by teaspoonfuls. Bake at 350 degrees F. for 15 minutes. Makes 2 dozen.

Oatmeal Peanut Butter Cookies

½ cup margarine
1 cup sugar
1 cup peanut butter
2 eggs
½ tsp. vanilla
1 tsp. salt
1 tsp. baking powder
2 cups rolled oats

Beat together margarine, sugar, peanut butter, eggs, and vanilla. Stir in remaining ingredients. Drop onto greased cookie sheet. Bake at 350 degrees F. for 10 to 15 minutes. Makes 2 dozen.
Note: This recipe uses no flour.

No-Bake Cookies

½ cup margarine
4 tbsp. cocoa or carob or combination of both
1 cup sugar
⅓ cup milk
3 cups rolled oats
½ cup peanut butter
1 tsp. vanilla
½ cup nuts (optional)
½ cup coconut (optional)

Combine margarine, carob/cocoa, sugar, and milk in saucepan. Heat to boiling. Remove from heat and stir in remaining ingredients. Drop by teaspoonfuls onto waxed paper to cool. Makes 2 dozen.

Oatmeal Cake

1¼ cups boiling water
1 cup rolled oats
½ cup margarine
1 cup brown sugar
2 eggs
1 tsp. vanilla
1½ cups whole wheat pastry flour
1 tsp. baking soda
¾ tsp. cinnamon
¼ tsp. nutmeg

In small bowl, pour boiling water over oats and let sit for 20 minutes. Meanwhile, beat margarine and brown sugar until fluffy. Blend in eggs and vanilla, then oat mixture. Stir in remaining ingredients. Mix well. Pour into well-greased, floured 9-inch square pan. Bake at 350 degrees F. for 50 minutes.

Oatmeal Bars

½ cup margarine
½ cup sugar
1 tsp. molasses
¼ tsp. baking powder
2 cups rolled oats

Melt margarine; stir in sugar and molasses. Cook and stir until sugar is melted. Stir in baking powder and oats. Spread in oiled 8-inch square baking pan. Bake at 350 degrees F. for 20 minutes. Cool thoroughly; cut into bars. Makes 9 bars.

Sesame Balls

¾ cup peanut butter
½ cup honey
1 tsp. vanilla
¾ cup non-instant powdered milk
1 cup rolled oats
½ cup sesame seeds
2 tbsp. boiling water

Combine peanut butter, honey, and vanilla. In separate bowl, combine dry milk and oats. Gradually add to peanut butter mixture. Blend in seeds and water. Form into 1-inch balls. Roll in additional seeds. Chill.

RICE

Nutritionally brown rice is far superior to white "enriched" rice. The reason is simple: virtually all the vitamins and minerals are in the outside covering, or bran. When the bran is removed to create white rice, most of the nutrition is also removed. Then the rice is "enriched" with a few artificial vitamins and minerals. How much better to just eat the rice in its natural form, with the natural vitamins, minerals, and "roughage" intact, the way nature produced it.

Short-grain brown rice, which cooks in about 15 minutes, and long-grain brown rice, which cooks in about 45 minutes, are both available at health food stores and food co-ops. Many grocery stores also carry brown rice.

If your family prefers white rice and balks at the idea of eating brown rice, you might consider buying what is called "converted rice." This rice has been through a process in which the nutrients are carried to the center of the grain before the bran is removed. Thus this rice is nearly as nutritious to eat as brown rice; it is, however, lower in iron, and it lacks the roughage. Converted rice always cooks up beautifully and turns out delicious.

Whereas white rice will store almost indefinitely, brown rice stores about two years and converted rice stores about ten years. Therefore, rice should be used and rotated if you have it in your food storage. In the following recipes, I have used converted rice. Brown rice will work just as well. Follow the instructions exactly for short-grain brown rice; adjust the amount of liquid and cooking time for long-grain rice, if uncooked rice is called for.

Rice Pudding

2 cups milk
⅓ cup honey
½ tsp. vanilla
¼ cup uncooked rice
2 eggs, beaten
Dash of salt

Combine all ingredients together in saucepan. Cook over medium heat until mixture boils, stirring constantly. Reduce heat, cover, and simmer gently until rice is tender, about 15 to 20 minutes. Cool. Serves 4.

Orange Rice Pudding

3 cups milk
½ cup uncooked rice
2 eggs
½ cup honey
½ tsp. salt
½ cup orange juice
2 tbsp. grated orange rind

In saucepan over low heat, cook milk and rice until rice is soft, about 15 minutes. Meanwhile, beat together remaining ingredients. Slowly add hot milk and rice to egg mixture, stirring constantly. Return to pan; simmer gently for about 5 minutes. Cool. (Mixture will thicken as it cools.) Serves 6.

Baked Rice

2 cups cooked rice
2 eggs
2 cups milk
2 tbsp. margarine
1 tbsp. soy sauce
1 cup cooked, chopped soy beans
    (or chopped peanuts)

Mix all ingredients together well. Pour into greased casserole. Bake at 350 degrees F. for 20 minutes or until set. Sprinkle with grated cheese last five minutes, if desired. Serves 4.

Rice Salad

2 cups cooked rice
1 to 2 carrots, finely diced
2 stalks celery, finely diced
½ cup raisins
Salad herbs to taste
Salt and pepper
Mayonnaise

Combine all ingredients. Stir in enough mayonnaise to moisten mixture. Chill to blend flavors. Serves 4.

Quiche Lorraine

1 medium onion, chopped
2 tbsp. green pepper, chopped
4 tbsp. margarine
1½ cups milk
3 eggs, beaten
¼ tsp. pepper
1 tbsp. parsley flakes
1 cup small curd cottage cheese
1 cup grated Swiss cheese

Sauté onion and green pepper in margarine until tender. Place in pie pan lined with a rice shell. Heat milk to scalding. Add small amounts of milk to egg; slowly stir in all the milk. Stir in remaining ingredients. Pour into shell. Bake at 325 degrees F. for 40 minutes or until set. Serves 4 to 6.

Variation: Substitute shredded Cheddar cheese for cottage cheese. Add sliced mushrooms, diced ham, crumbled bacon, or other ingredients to quiche before baking.

Rice Shell

A rice shell can be substituted for a regular pastry shell in many main dishes, particularly quiches. Simply pat 1½ cups cooked rice into a pie pan. Place in hot oven (about 400 degrees F.) for five minutes or until lightly browned. Fill with quiche mixture and bake as directed.

Spanish Rice

½ lb. ground beef
½ lb. mushrooms, sliced
1 medium onion, chopped
Oil
1 cup uncooked rice
1 1-lb. can tomatoes, cut up (or 2 cups)
½ tsp. oregano
½ tsp. basil
½ tsp. rosemary leaves
½ tsp. salt
Paprika

Brown ground beef, mushrooms, and onion in a little oil. Drain. Stir in remaining ingredients and bring to boil. Reduce heat and simmer gently for about 15 minutes or until rice is tender and liquid is absorbed. Serves 4.

Cashew Rice

½ cup chopped cashews
½ cup celery, diced
1 medium onion, chopped
1 4-oz. can mushroom stems and pieces, drained
3 tbsp. margarine
½ tsp. salt
½ tsp. thyme
Dash of pepper
1 cup rice
2 cups chicken stock

Sauté cashews, celery, onion, and mushrooms in margarine until onion is tender. Add remaining ingredients. Bring to boil. Cover and simmer gently for 15 minutes or until rice is tender. Serves 4.

Rice-Cheese Strata

3 cups cooked rice
1 cup cottage cheese
2 tbsp. pimiento
1 egg, beaten
¼ tsp. salt
½ cup celery, diced
½ onion, sliced
2 tbsp. margarine
2 cups shredded Cheddar cheese
Paprika
Tomato slices

Combine rice, cottage cheese, pimiento, egg, and salt. Cook celery and onion in margarine until onion is tender. Stir into rice mixture. Spoon half of the rice mixture into 2-quart casserole; sprinkle with half the cheese. Spoon remaining rice mixture in, then remaining cheese. Cover and bake at 375 degrees F. until hot. Sprinkle with paprika. Garnish with tomato slices. Serves 6.

Rice Puffs

1 egg
1 cup cooked rice
⅛ tsp. poultry seasoning
Dash of salt
½ cup grated Parmesan cheese
⅓ cup dry whole wheat bread crumbs

Beat egg; stir in rice, poultry seasoning, dash of salt, and cheese. Chill one hour or more in refrigerator. Shape into 1-inch balls. Roll in bread crumbs. Pour about 2 to 3 inches of oil in saucepan and heat to 375 degrees. Fry balls until golden brown on all sides. Makes 15 puffs.

Rice and Tomatoes

1 medium onion, chopped
½ green pepper, chopped
3 tbsp. margarine
1 1-lb. can stewed tomatoes
1 tsp. salt
Dash of pepper
3 cups cooked rice

Cook onion and green pepper in margarine until tender. Stir in remaining ingredients. Simmer gently until hot, about 15 minutes. Serves 4 to 6.

Rice Pilaf

¾ cup uncooked rice
1 small onion, chopped
1 cup fresh mushrooms, chopped
1 cup celery, chopped
2 tbsp. margarine
¼ tsp. allspice
3½ cups chicken stock
⅓ cup chopped nuts (optional)

Sauté rice, onion, mushrooms, and celery in margarine until onion is tender. Stir in remaining ingredients and heat to boiling. Pour into ungreased casserole and bake for 35 minutes at 350 degrees F. or until rice is tender. Serves 4.

Cracked Rice Cereal

2 cups milk
½ cup cracked rice (cracked in blender)
Dash of salt

Combine all ingredients in saucepan. Cook over medium heat, stirring constantly until mixture boils. Reduce heat and simmer for about 10 minutes. (Converted rice and short-grain brown rice take about 10 minutes to cook. Long-grain brown rice takes about 20 minutes to cook. A little more liquid may be added during cooking time, if necessary.) Serves 2 to 3.

MILLET

Millet is a grain that is sometimes called "poor man's rice." It looks like tiny yellow balls, and puffs up and becomes tender when cooked. Millet can be substituted for rice or noodles in many recipes. It is not expensive; in fact, it costs less than rice in health food stores, food co-ops, and home storage outlets. It is a rich source of protein, calcium, lecithin, and many other nutrients.

Millet can be cracked in the blender or ground in wheat grinders, but it tastes best cooked whole. It cooks like rice and takes about the same time to cook as short-grain brown rice or converted rice. Millet can also be sprouted.

Add millet to soups and casseroles, or combine equally with rice in puddings and main dishes.

Cracked Rice and Millet Cereal

2 cups milk
¼ cup cracked rice
¼ cup millet (cracked or whole)
Dash of salt

Combine all ingredients and stir over medium heat until boiling. Reduce heat and simmer for 10 minutes if millet is cracked, 15 if millet is whole. Serves 2 to 3.

Chicken Sausage Bake with Millet

2 cups chicken, cooked and chopped
1 lb. bulk sausage, browned
1½ cups cooked millet
1 medium onion, diced
1 cup gravy
Poultry seasoning to taste
Salt to taste
Biscuits (p. 16)

Combine chicken, sausage, millet, onion, gravy, and seasonings in greased baking dish. Top with biscuits. Bake at 350 degrees F. for 30 minutes or until biscuits are no longer doughy on the bottom.

Note: These measurements are approximate. Use more or less chicken, sausage, and millet as desired.

33

Millet Cheese Souffle

½ cup millet	Combine millet, water, salt, and dill
1½ cups water	seed in saucepan. Heat to boiling, then
¼ tsp. salt	reduce heat, cover, and simmer gently
¼ tsp. dill seed	for about 15 minutes. Remove from heat
2 eggs, separated	and cool slightly. Stir in egg yolks and
1 cup grated Swiss or Cheddar cheese	cheese. Gently fold in stiffly beaten
or mixture of both	egg whites, barely stirring. Pour into
1 tsp. parsley flakes	1½-quart greased casserole. Bake at
	350 degrees F. for 30 minutes. Serves 4.

Millet Soup

1 cup carrots, diced	Sauté carrots, celery, potatoes, and
1 cup celery, diced	onions in oil for 5 minutes. Add
1 cup potatoes, diced	remaining ingredients, except parsley.
1 cup onions, chopped	Simmer gently for about 35 minutes or
3 tbsp. oil	until vegetables are tender. Garnish
6 cups beef stock	with parsley.
1 cup canned tomatoes	
½ cup millet, uncooked	
3 tbsp. parsley flakes	

    Tip! Spike is a delicious seasoning available in health food stores and food co-ops. Try it in millet soup, other soups, vegetable dishes, and casseroles.

Sesame-Millet Fritters

½ cup milk	Blend milk, egg yolks, flour, and salt.
2 eggs, separated	Add millet and sesame seeds. Fold in
2 tbsp. whole wheat flour	stiffly beaten egg whites. Drop by
Dash of salt	tablespoonfuls onto hot, greased skillet.
⅔ cup cooked millet	Fry until golden brown; turn. Drain.
¼ cup roasted sesame seeds	Serve with gravy. Serves 4 to 6.

Corn and Millet Chowder

4 or more slices bacon	Cut bacon into pieces and cook with
⅔ cup chopped onion	onion in 4-quart saucepan until bacon
1 10-oz. can cream of mushroom soup	is crisp. Do not drain off fat. Add remaining
1 16-oz. can creamed corn	ingredients and bring to boil. Reduce heat
3 cups milk	and simmer gently until potatoes and millet
1 to 2 diced potatoes	are tender, about 15 to 20 minutes.
½ cup uncooked millet	Serves 4 to 6.
Salt to taste	
Dash of Worcestershire sauce	

Chicken-Cheese Soup with Millet

½ cup carrot, shredded
2 tbsp. onion, chopped
⅓ cup millet
2 tbsp. margarine
1 cup milk
1 cup water
1 10-oz. can cream of chicken soup
½ cup shredded Cheddar cheese
½ tsp. Worcestershire sauce

Cook carrot, onion, and millet in margarine until onion is soft. Stir in milk, water, and soup. Simmer gently for about 15 minutes, or until millet is tender. Remove from heat and stir in cheese and Worcestershire sauce, stirring until cheese melts. Serves 2 to 4.

Millet Casserole No. 1

1 cup millet
½ cup carrots, diced
½ cup celery, diced
1 tbsp. minced onion
2 tbsp. margarine
4 cups chicken stock
1 tsp. salad herbs
1 cup cooked chicken, diced

Sauté millet, carrots, celery, and onion in margarine until lightly browned. Add remaining ingredients; simmer for 20 minutes. Serves 4.

Millet Casserole No. 2

1 cup millet
1 medium onion, chopped
1 cup celery, chopped
2 tbsp. margarine
1 lb. ground beef
1 10-oz. can cream of mushroom soup or
    cream of celery soup
¼ tsp. sage
2 soup cans hot water
2 4-oz cans undrained mushrooms

Sauté millet, onion, and celery in margarine until lightly browned. Remove from heat. Brown meat and drain. Stir millet, vegetables, and remaining ingredients into meat. Pour into casserole. Bake at 350 degrees F. for 40 minutes, or until millet is tender. Serves 4.

Millet Casserole No. 3

2 cups water
1 cup millet
½ cup celery, chopped
2 cloves garlic, pressed
¼ tsp. poultry seasoning
½ cup onion, chopped
1 cup mushrooms, chopped
½ cup sunflower seeds
1 cup zucchini or yellow squash, chopped

Mix all ingredients well. Pour into greased casserole and bake for 1 to 1½ hours at 300 degrees F. Serves 4.

Millet-Seed Loaf

4 cups water
1 cup millet
3 4-oz. cans mushrooms, undrained
2 stalks celery, chopped
1 medium onion, chopped
1 envelope onion soup mix
1 10-oz. can cream of celery soup
1 cup sunflower seeds
½ cup sesame seeds
3 cups seed/nut mixture (sunflower seeds,
    sesame seeds, chopped soy nuts, chopped
    nuts, or combination of any above)

Boil water and millet. Cover and simmer gently for about 15 minutes or until millet is tender. Add remaining ingredients, except seed/nut mixture, and mix well. Pour into greased casserole and top with seed/nut mixture. Bake at 300 degrees F. for 30 minutes or until heated through. Serves 4 to 6.

Tuna and Millet Bisque

½ cup onion, chopped
½ cup millet
2 tbsp. margarine
1 10-oz. can cream of mushroom soup
1 10-oz. can cream of potato soup
1 10-oz. pkg. frozen mixed vegetables, cooked
1 6-oz. can tuna, drained
2 soup cans milk
2½ tsp. lemon juice
½ tsp. hot sauce
Salt to taste

Cook onion and millet in margarine until onion is tender. Add remaining ingredients, plus one cup water. Bring to boil. Reduce heat and simmer gently 15 to 20 minutes. Salt to taste. Makes 8 cups.

Puffed Cauliflower, Cheese, and Millet

½ cup margarine
2 tbsp. whole wheat flour
1 cup milk
½ tsp. salt
Dash of pepper
½ cup dry whole wheat bread crumbs
1 cup cooked millet
3 eggs, separated
1 cup grated cheese
1 medium head of cauliflower, cooked
Buttered bread crumbs (optional)

Melt margarine and stir in flour; cook for 1 minute. Gradually stir in milk, stirring until smooth. Stir in salt, pepper, and bread crumbs. Then add millet, egg yolks, cheese, and cauliflower. Fold in stiffly beaten egg whites. Pour into greased casserole and bake at 400 degrees F. for about 30 minutes. Sprinkle with buttered bread crumbs last 10 minutes, if desired. Serves 4.

Baked Chicken Squares

3 cups cubed, cooked chicken
2 cups soft bread crumbs
2 cups cooked millet
1 tsp. salt
2 cups chicken broth
1 cup milk
4 eggs, beaten
Mushroom gravy or sauce

Layer chicken, bread crumbs, and millet in 12x8-inch baking dish. Mix salt, broth, and milk together. Add eggs and beat. Pour over chicken mixture. Bake at 325 degrees F. for 50 minutes, or until set. Cut into squares. Serve with mushroom gravy or sauce. (Use a package of mushroom gravy mix, or heat some cream of mushroom soup with ½ can water; add a small can of mushrooms, drained.) Serves 4.

CORN

Corn can be purchased at health food stores or food co-ops and ground in a grinder at home. Check the manufacturer's instructions; corn should be ground on a coarse setting. Cornmeal can also be purchased already ground in the stores. Look for *stone-ground* cornmeal. Metal grinders get very hot, and the heat destroys many of the nutrients, making stone-ground corn or wheat, or any grain, more desirable than grain ground in a metal grinder.

Basic Corn Bread

1½ cups cornmeal
½ cup whole wheat flour
2 tsp. baking powder
1 tsp. baking soda
1 tsp. salt
¼ cup cooking oil
1½ cups milk (or use ¾ cup water and
    ¾ cup yogurt)
2 eggs

Beat together all ingredients until smooth. Pour into a greased 8-inch square pan and bake at 450 degrees F. for 25 to 30 minutes. Serves 6 to 8.

Corn Dogs

1 egg, beaten
1 cup milk
½ cup cornmeal
⅓ cup sugar
¼ tsp. salt
1 cup whole wheat flour
1 tsp. baking powder
12 hot dogs

Mix together all the ingredients. Cook 12 hot dogs and drain, then pat dry. Dip hot dogs in batter, then fry in oil at 375 degrees F. until browned on all sides. Makes 12 corn dogs.

Vegetable Scrapple

3½ cups boiling water
½ cup onion, chopped
½ cup carrot, chopped
¼ cup green pepper, finely diced
2 cups cornmeal
2 eggs
1 tsp. salt
1 cup soy nuts or peanuts, chopped

Bring water to boil and add onion, carrot, and green pepper. Simmer for 2 minutes. Slowly stir in cornmeal, stirring constantly. Remove from heat. With wire whip, blend in eggs, salt, then peanuts or soy nuts. Pour into greased 4¼x8½-inch loaf pan. Bake at 350 degrees F. for one hour. Remove from oven and chill in refrigerator several hours. With sharp knife, cut into slices. Heat oil in skillet, and fry on both sides until browned. Serves 4 to 6.

Gnocchi

Prepare and cook vegetable scrapple as above. Instead of pouring into loaf pan, turn mixture into a greased 8-inch square pan; bake at 350 degrees F. for about 40 minutes. Chill in refrigerator several hours. With sharp knife, cut into squares and lay in greased baking dish. Dot with margarine, and sprinkle with ½ cup grated Cheddar cheese. Bake at 425 degrees F. for about 10 minutes or until hot. Serves 4.

Corn Pancakes

1¼ cups water
1 egg
2 tbsp. oil
½ cup whole wheat flour
½ cup cornmeal
1 tbsp. baking powder
1 tsp. salt

Combine water, egg, and oil. Stir in remaining ingredients. Bake on hot griddle. (Corn pancakes are especially good when served with real maple syrup.) Serves 4.

Cheese Corn Muffins

1 cup cornmeal
1 tsp. salt
1 tsp. baking powder
1 tsp. honey
1 cup buttermilk (or ½ cup yogurt and
    ½ cup water)
2 tbsp. oil
1 egg, beaten
¼ to ½ cup grated Cheddar cheese

Mix together dry ingredients. Combine remaining ingredients except cheese. Blend into dry ingredients. Pour into well-greased muffin tins. Sprinkle with cheese. Bake at 425 degrees F. for 15 minutes. Makes 1 dozen.

Cornmeal and Ground Beef Casserole

½ cup cornmeal
½ cup cold water
1 cup hot water
1 tbsp. oil
1 medium onion, chopped
2 cups ground beef/wheat mixture
    (see p. 7.) or 1 lb. ground beef
1 tsp. salt
1 egg, beaten
1 tsp. savory
1 tbsp. parsley flakes
3 tomatoes, sliced

Blend cornmeal with cold water until smooth. Blend in hot water; set aside. In skillet heat oil and sauté onion. Stir in cornmeal mixture, meat, salt, egg, savory, and parsley. Turn mixture into a well-greased casserole. Top with sliced tomatoes. Bake at 350 degrees F. for 20 minutes. Serves 6.

Corn Tortillas No. 1

1 cup boiling water
1 cup cornmeal
2 to 2½ cups whole wheat flour
½ tsp. salt

Pour boiling water over cornmeal and let sit about 10 minutes. Mix flour and salt, adding enough flour to make a kneadable dough. Knead 5 minutes. Let sit 5 minutes. Pinch off a piece about 2 inches in diameter. Roll out on floured board to about 4 inches in diameter. Cook on hot griddle for about 2 minutes on each side. Makes 1 dozen.

Corn Tortillas No. 2

1½ cups cold water
½ cup cornmeal
1 cup whole wheat flour
½ tsp. salt
1 egg

Beat all ingredients together until smooth. Pour ¼ cup batter on hot 8-inch skillet, lightly greased. Lift pan to rotate to form a very thin tortilla. Cook 2 minutes. Turn to other side and cook. Makes 1 dozen.

Tostados

Corn tortillas (above)
Pinto beans, cooked, mashed, and
    seasoned with chili powder
Monterey Jack cheese, shredded
Lettuce, shredded
Onion, finely diced
Tomato, diced
Avocado, sliced (optional)

Cook tortillas, as above. (If they have been cooked ahead, heat them up for about 5 minutes in medium oven.) Spread with mashed pinto beans and sprinkle with cheese. Heat in oven until cheese melts. Top with remaining ingredients.

Hush Puppies

2¼ cups cornmeal
1 tsp. salt
2 tbsp. finely diced onion
¾ tsp. baking soda
1½ cups buttermilk (or use ¾ cup water and
    ¾ cup yogurt)

Mix together cornmeal, salt, onion, and baking soda. Stir in liquid. Drop by teaspoonfuls onto hot oil. Fry until golden brown on all sides, about 2 minutes. Makes 2 dozen.

Bacon and Cheese Polenta

Follow recipe for Basic Corn Bread, adding ½ pound bacon, cooked and crumbled; 1 cup shredded cheese; 1 onion, sautéed in bacon grease; and substituting ¼ cup bacon grease for the ¼ cup cooking oil.

POPCORN

Unbuttered popcorn is low in calories, inexpensive, and a delicious snack. Popcorn can also be ground in wheat grinder and used for cornmeal. In this section are some variations of basic popcorn.

Parmesan Popcorn

Cook popcorn; pour on melted butter or margarine. Generously sprinkle with Parmesan cheese; stir.

Seasoned Popcorn

Sprinkle seasoned salt over buttered or unbuttered popcorn.

Caramel Corn

½ cup margarine
½ cup honey
Dash of maple flavoring (optional)
4 quarts popped popcorn (or more), cooled

Melt margarine and honey. Bring to boil and cook for about 1 to 2 minutes. Remove from heat and stir in maple flavoring. Pour over popcorn and stir. Let cool.

Marshmallow Popcorn Balls

6 tbsp. margarine
3 cups miniature marshmallows
½ 3-oz. pkg. raspberry gelatin
3 quarts popped popcorn, unsalted

Melt margarine in top of double boiler over boiling water; add marshmallows and melt. Blend in dry gelatin. Pour over popcorn, and mix well with buttered hands. Form into balls.

SOYBEANS

Nutritionists class soybeans as one of the five great protein foods. Weight for weight, soybeans have one and one-half times as much protein as cheese, twice as much protein as fish or meat, three times as much protein as eggs, and eleven times as much protein as milk. Two pounds of low-fat soy flour contain as much protein as 5 pounds of steak, 5 dozen eggs, 15 quarts of milk, or 4 pounds of cheese.

Soybeans have much more to offer than protein; they are also rich in vitamins and minerals. They are an excellent and inexpensive way to supplement your meal ideas.

To cook soybeans, pour them into ice cube trays and fill with water. Place in freezer overnight. Next morning, put beans and ice in pan and bring to boil. Simmer gently 2 to 3 hours. Or soak overnight in refrigerator, and next morning simmer gently 4 to 5 hours.

Soybeans can also be sprouted and used in a variety of ways. Be careful, though —cooked or sprouted beans spoil easily. Uncooked or unsprouted beans will keep indefinitely.

Soy flour may be purchased in health food stores or food co-ops. It is a very nutritious flour. Soy flour can be substituted for part of the regular flour called for in baking in many recipes. Because of its light color, many baked goods look as though they have been made with white flour. Add soy flour to white bread, but avoid using it in wheat bread.

Do *not* grind soybeans in a stone grinder unless you first read manufacturer's instructions. Soybeans are oily and can gum up the stones.

Soybean Sandwiches

Mix equal parts cooked, mashed soybeans with tuna, chicken, or hard-cooked eggs. Mix in onion, pickle, mayonnaise, salt, and pepper. Refrigerate what is not eaten immediately.

Soybean Pie

1 ½ cups soybeans, cooked and ground
1 ½ cups milk
¾ cup evaporated milk
1 cup sugar
1 tsp. molasses
1 ½ tsp. ginger
½ tsp. cloves
½ tsp. nutmeg
¼ tsp. cinnamon
1 tbsp. grated lemon rind
2 eggs
Unbaked 9-inch pie shell

Combine ground soybeans and milk in blender or food processor. Blend in remaining ingredients until very smooth and pour into pie shell. Bake at 400 degrees F. for 45 minutes or until knife inserted in middle comes out clean. Serve with whipped cream. (Tastes similar to pumpkin pie.)

Soybean Patties

2 cups soybeans, cooked and chopped
2 cups cooked rice
2 tbsp. oil
1 medium onion, diced
2 tsp. soy sauce
½ tsp. garlic salt
½ cup whole wheat bread crumbs

Put soybeans in blender and add enough water to blend into a stiff paste. Pour into bowl, using spatula to remove. Blend with remaining ingredients, except bread crumbs. Place in greased baking pan, sprinkle with bread crumbs, and bake at 350 degrees F. until lightly browned. Makes 20 patties.

Soy Nuts

Soak soybeans in water for 12 to 24 hours. Pat dry. Heat oil in deep-fryer to 350 degrees F. Fry soybeans for about 7 minutes or until golden brown and crisp. Do not burn. Salt to taste.

POWDERED MILK

Powdered milk is more economical to use than fresh milk, has fewer calories (except for fresh skim milk), and has virtually all the nutritional value of fresh milk. Many families do not care for the taste of powdered milk. However, when used in cooking and baking, the powdered milk taste cannot be detected. Use reconstituted milk in puddings, custards, gravies, casseroles, soups, and other recipes.

In some recipes the milk does not need to be reconstituted. Simply add dry milk solids to the dry ingredients and replace the milk called for with an equal amount of water.

I have the following chart posted on my cupboard. Whenever I am using a recipe that calls for milk, whether ¼ cup or 6 cups, I use the chart as a guide, and mix up exactly as much as I need. Often I estimate, using slightly more milk solids than necessary. It just adds a little more protein, calcium, and other nutrients to the recipe!

To yield:	Use this much non-instant milk:	Use this much instant milk:
2 qts.	1⅓ cups	⅔ cups
1 qt.	⅔ cups	1⅓ cups
3 cups	½ cup	1 cup
2 cups	⅓ cup	⅔ cup
1 cup	8 tsp.	⅓ cup
½ cup	4 tsp.	8 tsp.
¼ cup	2 tsp.	4 tsp.

You will notice that it takes twice as much instant powdered milk to make the same quantity of non-instant powdered milk.

Sweetened Condensed Milk

1¾ cup sugar
1 cup boiling water
½ cup margarine, softened
4 cups instant or 2 cups non-instant
    powdered milk

Dissolve sugar in boiling water; remove from heat. Stir in margarine, mix well with wire whisk or electric beaters, beat in milk, 1 cup at a time. Store in refrigerator. Keeps 1 month. Makes 3½ cups.

Creamy Vanilla Pudding

1/3 cup sugar
2 tbsp. cornstarch
1/8 tsp. salt
2 cups milk
2 egg yolks, slightly beaten
2 tsp. vanilla
2 tbsp. margarine

Combine sugar, cornstarch, and salt in saucepan. Gradually stir in milk. Stirring constantly, bring mixture to boil; boil 1 minute. *Slowly* stir in about half of pudding mixture into egg yolks. Pour egg yolk mixture back into saucepan and boil 1 minute. Stir in vanilla and margarine. Cool. Serves 4.

Custard

2 eggs, beaten well
1/4 cup honey
1/2 tsp. vanilla
Dash of salt
1 1/2 cups milk

Combine all ingredients until well blended. Pour into 4 custard cups. Arrange in skillet with tight-fitting lid. Pour hot water up to the level of the custard mixture. Cover and bring to boil. Turn off heat and let custard stand, covered, 10 minutes. Refrigerate. (Do *not* allow water to boil into custard mixture.) Serves 4.

Quick Butterscotch Pudding

1/3 cup honey
1/4 cup cornstarch
1/8 tsp. salt
2 3/4 cups milk
2 tbsp. margarine
1 tsp. maple flavoring

Combine honey, cornstarch, salt, and milk in saucepan. Stirring constantly, bring to boil. Boil 1 minute, then remove from heat. Stir in margarine and maple flavoring. Cover with plastic wrap to avoid skin that forms on top while cooling. Makes 3 cups.

Thin Pancakes

1 1/2 cups water
3 eggs
1 1/3 cups whole wheat flour
1/2 cup non-instant powdered milk
1 tsp. salt

Combine all ingredients in blender, and blend on high speed until all ingredients are well mixed. Melt butter or margarine in skillet; pour enough batter into pan to make about a 5-inch pancake. Cook until browned, then turn over and brown on other side. Good served with butter and syrup, or filled with fruit and whipped cream and roll up. Makes twelve 5-inch pancakes.

Yogurt

1 cup non-instant powdered milk 1 qt. warm water 3 tbsp. plain yogurt	Combine milk and water and heat to scalding. Cool to barely lukewarm (about 100 degrees F.). Blend in yogurt. Pour into yogurt maker and "cook" for 10 hours. Makes 1 quart. *Note:* Yogurt can be "cooked" anywhere that a temperature of 100 to 120 degrees F. can be maintained. You may use a dehydrator, oven, thermos, and so on. Also, 1 tsp. unflavored gelatin may be added to milk before scalding, if desired, to help yogurt set up thicker.

Tip! Yogurt may be mixed with equal parts water and used in place of buttermilk. Yogurt may also be used in place of sour cream in many recipes. Try mixing half sour cream and half yogurt to serve on baked potatoes. Fewer calories!

Yogurt Popsicles No. 1

1 6-oz. can frozen orange juice 1 1/2 cans water 1 1/2 to 2 cups yogurt	Combine orange juice and water until smooth. Stir in yogurt. Freeze in molds or 3-oz. paper cups with a spoon in each. Makes 10.

Yogurt Popsicles No. 2

1/2 cup water 1 3-oz. envelope gelatin, any flavor 1/4 cup sugar 2 cups yogurt	Heat water, gelatin, and sugar until gelatin and sugar dissolve. Add yogurt. Freeze in paper cups or molds. Makes 10.

Yogurt Burgers

1 lb. ground beef 1/4 cup onion, chopped 1/2 cup catsup 2 tsp. vinegar 1 tsp. salt 1/2 tsp. dry mustard 1/2 cup yogurt 4 hamburger buns	Brown ground beef with onion and drain. Stir in catsup, vinegar, salt, and dry mustard. Cover and simmer over low heat for 10 minutes. Remove from heat. Stir in yogurt. Serve over hamburger buns. Serves 4.

Yogurt Cream Cheese

Pour 4 cups homemade or purchased yogurt into a cheesecloth-lined sieve. Let drain several hours or overnight into a bowl. Only a water-like substance should drain out, leaving a thick cream cheese behind. This cream cheese can be used in many recipes calling for cream cheese. It is still tart, though, like yogurt.

Yogurt Cheese Cake

2 cups yogurt cream cheese
¼ cup milk
3 eggs, separated
1 tsp. vanilla
⅔ cup sugar
1 graham cracker crust

Combine yogurt cream cheese, milk, egg yolks, vanilla, and sugar until smooth. Fold in stiffly beaten egg whites. Pour into graham cracker crust and bake at 350 degrees F. for 30 minutes or until set. Chill.

Peach Dessert

1 cup fresh peaches, peeled and sliced
1 tbsp. lemon juice
¼ cup sugar
1 cup yogurt
2 tsp. grated orange rind
Dash of almond extract

In large bowl, combine peaches, lemon juice, and sugar. Toss lightly. Combine yogurt, orange rind, and almond extract. Mix well. Pour yogurt mixture over peaches; mix gently but thoroughly. Chill. Serves 2 to 3.

Favorite Vegetable Dip

½ cup mayonnaise
½ cup yogurt
Parsley flakes, dried
Onion powder
Garlic powder
Parmesan cheese
Celery seed
Dillweed
Other herbs and spices, as desired

Combine mayonnaise and yogurt with flavorings as desired. Chill to blend flavors. Use as a vegetable dip, as a ranch-style dressing for salads, or in coleslaw. Makes 1 cup.

"Tootsie Rolls"

½ cup honey
¼ cup cocoa
½ cup instant powdered milk or ¼ cup
   non-instant powdered milk
½ tsp. vanilla

Cook honey to hard ball stage. Remove from heat. Stir in cocoa, milk, and vanilla. Blend well with wire whisk. Cool enough to handle. Roll out to pencil size; cut in desired lengths. (Candy hardens quickly.) Wrap in waxed paper.

Macaroons

1 cup sweetened condensed milk
1 8-oz. pkg. shredded coconut
1 tsp. vanilla

Combine all ingredients. Add more coconut if necessary to make as stiff a dough as possible. Drop onto well-greased cookie sheet. Bake at 350 degrees F. for 10 to 12 minutes or until golden brown. Cool slightly, then remove from pan to cool completely.

Yummy Apple Salad

4 large apples, peeled and shredded
1 tsp. lemon juice
4 tsp. sugar
½ cup yogurt, or more
½ cup chopped nuts, or more

Combine apples with lemon juice. Set aside. Blend sugar into yogurt and stir into apples. Stir in nuts. Chill. Serves 6 to 8.

INDEX